T0381360

DAN AND JAN; FAY AND JAY; MY PUP; AND MY DOG

ANOTHER FOUR-SHORT-STORY BOOK

ANGELA K. PAGE

AuthorHouse™
1663 Liberty Drive
Bloomington, IN 47403
www.authorhouse.com
Phone: 1 (800) 839-8640

Published by AuthorHouse 07/10/2019

ISBN: 978-1-7283-1083-1 (sc)
ISBN: 978-1-7283-1084-8 (hc)
ISBN: 978-1-7283-1082-4 (e)

Library of Congress Control Number: 2019942616

Print information available on the last page.

Contents

DAN AND JAN

By Angela K. Page
Illustrated by Wilma Purcell

Word List

1. an	2. ban	3. Dan	4. and	5. badly (bad/ly)	6. in
7. it	8. if	9. of	10. is	11. this	12. his
13. as	14. glass	15. has	16. have	17. haven (hav/en	18. taken (tak/en)
19. shaken (shak/en)	20. or	21. nor	22. for	23. before (be/fore)	24. metaphor (met/a/phor)
25. out	26. stout	27. shout	28. clout	29. bout	30. about (a/bout)
31. far	32. jar	33. star	34. tar	35. are	36. hide
37. ride	38. bide	39. abide (a/bide)	40. book	41. look	42. took
43. shook	44. oops	45. ooze	46. loop	47. scoop	48. fun
49. bun	50. hungry (hun/gry)	51. by	52. shy	53. why	54. cry

Word List

55. ice	56. nice	57. mice	58. lice	59. rice	60. entice (en/tice)
61. the	62. then	63. them	64. they	65. that	66. here
67. there	68. where	69. dump	70.bump	71. jump	72. thump
73. real	74. meal	75. mean	76. eat	77. beat	78. feet
79. ask	80. task	81. fast	82. past	83. last	84. mask
85. our	86. hour	87. scour	88. round	89. around (a/round)	

Word List

90. tower	91. shower	92. brown	93. town	94.crown	95. frown
96. her	97. flower (flow/er)	98. over (o/ver)	99. other (oth/er)	100. another (an/oth/er)	101. perfectly (per/fect/ly)
102. utterly (ut/ter/ly)	103. altogether al/to/geth/er	104. totally (to/tal/ly)	105. absolutely (ab/so/lute/ly)	106. rain	107. train
108. brain	109. refrain (re/frain)	110.aim	111. tame		

It's Rudimentary
Dan and Jan by Angela K. Page
Copyright© 2018-2019/All Rights Reserved
Created at Empowering Learning Institute

Here are Dan and Jan. He
is Dan and she is Jan.

Dan and Jan have fun in the sun.

Dan and Jan look far for another big star.

Dan and Jan see the dog that loves to bark and wags her tail.

Dan and Jan ride in a car over the hard dark tar.

Dan and Jan use a spoon to scoop peanut butter from a tan glass jar.

Dan and Jan jumped over a steep bump found on the brown ground.

Dan and Jan are shy and try not
to cry, when they treat a sore
on Dan's tiny knee. Dan and Jan
still treat with heat the scar on
Dan's tiny knee and are also
careful about their tiny knees.

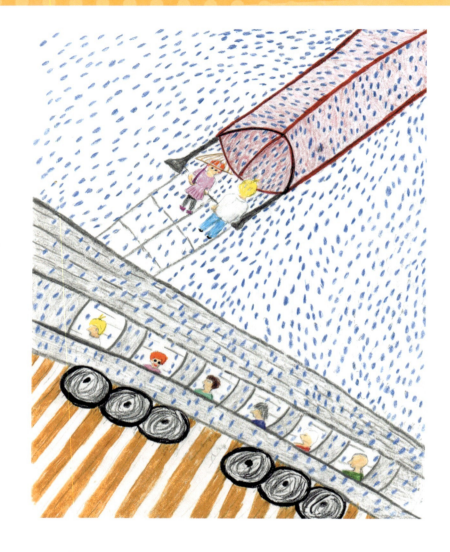

Dan and Jan stay out of the rain.

Dan and Jan also ride in a fast train.

Dan and Jan look hungrily at the very nice cook.

Dan and Jan are fed their evening meal four hours before they go to sleep on their red new bed.

A. Complete each sentence with the correct term based on the story. Answer the other questions in a complete sentence or sentences.

1. Here (is/are) Dan and Jan.

2. Dan and Jan jump over the (bump, dump).

3. Dan and Jan ride in a fast (plane, train).

4. Dan and Jan look hungrily (hun/gri/ly) at the (book, cook).

5. Dan and Jan have their evening meal (four, five) hours before they go to bed.

6. Dan and Jan (are/is) careful about the (tar/ scar) on Dan's (tiny, bony) knee.

7. Dan and Jan ride in a (car, shark) over the dark (tar/ ground).

8. Who are the main characters or subjects in the story? Tell why.

9. Main Idea Identification/Tell the main idea of this story (sto/ry) and give two or more supporting details.

10. Formulate (For/mu/late) an Alternate (Al/ter/nate) Story Ending/ How did this story end? As an author (au/thor) write another (a/ noth/er) story ending.

11. Vocabulary Development/Use pictures and story content to tell what "tar" means?

12. Practice (Prac/tice) reciting (re/cit/ing) these blends whether (wheth/er) they are double vowels and consonants and consonant-vowel blends: "rh"; "ba"; "sc"; "am"; "tion"; "oo"; "ow"; "gr"; "br"; "st"; "sl"; "ai"; "oi"; "or"; "um"; "au"; "at"; "ei"; "ly"; "ph", and "ment".

13. What sound does the "y" make in "shy", "cry", "why", "try", and "story"?

The End

FAY AND JAY

By Angela K. Page
Illustrated by Morgan A. Page

Word List

1. I	2. A	3. an	4. am	5. on
6. in	7. be	8. we	9. see	10. to
11. too	12. two	13. the	14. then	15. them
16. they	17. bay	18. say	19. play	20. stay
21. stay	22. tease	23. please	24. cheese	25. meet
26. meat	27. tower	28. our	29. flour	30. flower
31. chief	32. niece	33. belief (be/lief)	34. believe be/lieve	35. achieve (a/chieve)
36. receive (re/ceive)	37. receiver (re/ceiv/er)	38. vein	39. eight	40. weigh
41. weight	42. night	43. tight	44. right	45. plight
46. flight				

I am Fay.

I am Jay.

We go to the bay

to play in the hay.

Come night says Zay,

"Please, stay and play!"

Come day says Fay,

"We will be on our way."

A. Complete each sentence with the correct word based on the content of the story. Also, answer the following (fol/low/ing) questions in a complete sentence or sentences.

1. Fay and Jay (is/are) the main characters in this story. Which verb was selected? Tell why.

2. Fay and Jay are going to the (bay, stable).

3. Zay tells Fay and Jay to stay and (lay, play).

4. Fay tells Zay they will go back the next (day, night).

5. List all vowels and consonants.

6. **Phonemic Recognition/**Practice reciting the double consonant-vowel blend: "ble". Recite this word 3 times: "able (a/ble)".

7. Recite the terms: "night", "tight", and "right" three times. How would you describe the sound of the double-consonant blend "gh"?

8. From the word list on page 18, find the "double-vowel blends" with the "long e" and "long a" sounds.

9. Identify a set of homophones from the word list.

10. Synonyms (Syn/o/nyms) are terms with similar (sim/i/lar) meanings. What do you think antonyms (is/are)? What is an antonym for "night"?

11. Tell another character in this story.

12. What is the main idea of this story? Tell one supporting detail.

13. **Formulate an Alternate Story Ending/** How did this story end? As an author, write an alternate (al/ter/nate) end for this story.

The End

MY PUP

By Angela K. Page
Illustrated by Morgan Page

Word List

1. A	2. is/his	3. it	4. in	5. ink	6.drinks
7. my	8. by	9. sky	10. up	11. pup	12. if
13.sniff	14.under (un/der)	15. run	16. ran	17. low	18. blow
19.slow (slow/ly)	20. hay	21.say	22.away (a/way)	23.bake	24. cake
25.take	26.bump	27.jump	28.thump	29. eat	30. heat
31. toy	32. boy	33. joy	34.wing	35.swing	

Word List

36.thing	37. thinking (think/ing)	38. thinker (think/er)	39. toes	40. woes	41. foes
42. am	43. jam	44. scam	45. name	46. tame	47. fame
48. few	49. pew	50. blew	51. threw	52. happy (hap/py)	53. taffy (taf/fy)
54. tacky (tack/y)	55. or	56. for	57. nor	58. torn	59. scorn

It's Rudimentary
My Pup by Angela K. Page

My pup is a boy.

My pup jumps for joy.

My pup swings his toys.

My pup's name is Zup, and he drinks from his cup.

My pup eats bugs.

My pup loves hugs.

My pup runs slowly.

My pup bumps low.

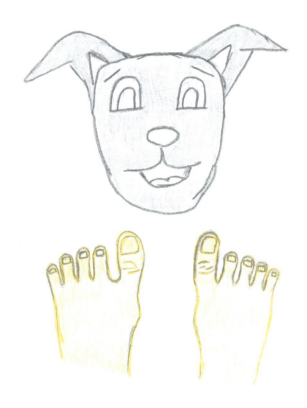

My pup sniffs toes.

Pew!

My pup takes away my woes
to make me happy.

A. Complete each sentence with the correct word based on the story.

1.   My pup is a (boy, girl).

2.   My pup eats (bugs, slugs).

3.   My pup runs (fast, slowly).

4.   My pup sniffs (fingers, toes).

5.   My pup takes away my (foes, woes).

B. Answer the following (fol/low/ing) questions (ques/tions) in complete sentences.

6.   What is the main subject or character in this story?

7.   Tell one action (verb) of the pup Zup, in this story.

8.   Adverbs are terms that describe the (actions or verbs) in a sentence. Inquiry (in/quir/y) number 7, you identified (i/den/ti/fied) a verb. Identify (i/den/ti/fy) the adverbs on pages 38 and 39.

9.   Choose two terms from this page to write them in syllables and tell how many syllables are heard. For example, how many syllables are heard in identify (i/den/ti/fy).

10. Tell the main idea of this story. The main idea is one general statement that describes what the subject is doing in the story.

11. **Making Inferences/** Do you think Zup is a happy or sad pup? Use story content to explain (ex/plain).

12. Use the story content to tell what you think "woes" mean and a synonym (syn/o/nym).

The End

MY DOG

By Angela K. Page
Illustrations by Morgan Page and Wilma Purcell

Word List

1. a	2. an	3. and	4. by	5. my	6. it	7. in	8. on
9. is	10. his	11. as	12. has	13. be	14. he	15. we	16. she
17. see	18. seek	19. big	20. dig	21. jig	22. wig	23. bun	24. fun
25. run	26. up	27. pup	28. Ed	29. fed	30. red	31. bed	32. bog
33. dog	34. fog	35. hog	36. jog	37. log	38. smog	39. cot	40. hot
41. over o/ver	42. other oth/er	43. tether teth/er	44. mother moth/er	45. father fa/ther	46. under un/der	47. wonder won/der	48. wander wan/der

Word List

49. lot	50. hay	51. say	52. play	53. stay	54. of	55. if	56. sniff
57. arm	58. farm	59. barn	60. dark	61. sea	62. see	63. bee	64. tree
65. three	66. them	67. then	68. they	69. the	70. dish	71. fish	72. wish
73. bide	74. hide	75. side	76. to	77. too	78. two	79. there	80. their
81. where	82. when	83. hen	84. old	85. sold	86. bold	87. fold	88. told
89. hold	90. mold	91. ties	92. flies	93. lies			

It's Rudimentary

My dog is fun.

**My dog runs up the hill
under the sun.**

**He sips from his dish
and sees a red fish.**

My dog jogs to the bog to sniff a green frog.

He lies on the log when
there is lots of smog.

My dog plays with his
pal, the big old hog.

They stay on the farm to play hide-and-seek in the dark and fog.

A. Answer the following questions.

1. The dog in the story is not fun: True or False.

2. What does the dog see while sipping from the dish?

3. What does the dog sniff?

4. Use clues from the story to tell if the dog is a boy or girl.

5. Who is the dog's pal and what, where, and when do they play?

6. Formulating/Give the dog a name. Tell how you came up with this name.

7. Recite these terms: "to", "two (2)", and "too". They are homophones. What are homophones? Identify (I/den/ti/fy) two (2) more sets of homophones from the word list.

8. Practice reciting the following blends whether they are double vowels and consonants, and consonant-vowel: "th"; "dr";" "wh"; "ay"; "ee"; "ea"; "ew"; "un"; "up"; "pl"; "ar"; "er"; "sh", "ch"; "og"; "sw"; "an"; "ie"; "py";"ed"; "ig"; and "ip".

The End

Reading Activities

There is much to do to model how "reading is not passive, but very active and engaging." First, the children can be animatedly read to while pointing to the words as they are heard. To motivate attentiveness, pause exhibiting the five-finger count in the middle of the sentence, allowing the young reader to recite the word after the count. Of course, the young reader is expected to respond to the questions following each short story. Some of the responses can be expressed orally, while the others are written in a complete sentence or sentences. To build writing skills, the young erudite can be directed to use part of the question to start-off the written response. Know your reader to plan properly the activities that are completed during one setting. During one reading setting for example, the focus could be reciting and timing how fluently the terms are read from the word list. To hand-clapping and feet-beating, focus on reading the words in syllables.

For phonemic activities, the word list can also be used to determine how well the young reader recognizes and identifies the sounds of vowels, consonants, and blends. The goal here is not to test how well the reader memorizes the spelling of these words. For example, enunciate emphasizing syllables. Provide clues such as "this word has a double vowel with a long vowel sound or a double consonant that is silent." The young reader can pinpoint the phonology of the rhymes; specifically, the identification of the alphabets, blends and the associated sounds.

The young reader can devise a word frequency list, especially indicating the frequency and the reason to use: articles such as "a, an, and the"; adjective and adverb "their and there"; the auxiliary verbs such as "is and are", and other selected words that are chosen for this activity. A literary discussion is followed to determine the ability of the young erudite to "self-discover" and not the memorization of grammarian rules and syntactical patterns. Through engaging activities, the young reader is encouraged to make self-discoveries so learning is meaningful, and is not inclined to be forgetful.

With adult assistance, reading rates can be computed. To express the reading rate as the number of words read in 15 or 30 seconds, the young reader records the number of words read while timed. The adult divides the number of words read by .25 or .30 of a minute: the equivalence of 15 or 30 seconds. Imagine how exciting it is for young readers to track reading rates. Just have fun so that the young scholars are motivated to **"Read, Read, and Read!"**

About the Author

Angela Page is a doctoral, hands-on learner and has over 30 years as an educator. Angela is also a Master of Education graduate of Howard University's School of Education in Washington, D.C. She has received many accolades from *Outstanding Educator, Women in Science, and Leadership Awards to the Maryland State Presidential award for Excellence in Mathematics and Science Teaching*. After retiring from Prince George's County Public Schools System as a science teacher, she started **Empowering Learning Institute**. It is an institute where young scholars, scientists, mathematical problem-solvers, and junior engineers are nurtured. It is also an institute where Angela receives inspiration to create her children's books. Angela creates these rudimentary reading materials for the novice and for those students who have reading challenges. In her materials, a basic word list is included to practice breaking-down terms into syllables, and sounding out and reading terms similar to the words in the story to develop reading confidence and fluency. She also encourages vocabulary development through the discussion of content clues. Angela Page now lives in Clinton, Maryland with her lovable, supportive family and community.

Printed in the United States
By Bookmasters